Where Do Babies Come From?

A Guide for the Christian Family

boys ages 6–8

CONCORDIA PUBLISHING HOUSE • SAINT LOUIS

Book 2 of the Learning about Sex Series
The titles in the series:

Book 1: Why Boys and Girls Are Different

Book 2: Where Do Babies Come From?

Book 3: How You Are Changing

Book 4: Sex and the New You

Book 5: Love, Sex, and God

Book 6: How to Talk Confidently with Your Child about Sex

Acknowledgments

We wish to thank all medical, child development, and family life consultants who have assisted in the development, updating, and revising of the Learning about Sex series.

Copyright © 1982, 1988, 1995, 1998, 2008, 2015 Concordia Publishing House
3558 S. Jefferson Ave., St. Louis, MO 63118-3968
1-800-325-3040 • cph.org

From text originally written by Ruth Hummel

Illustrations by Janet McDonnell

Scripture quotations from the ESV® Bible (The Holy Bible, English Standard Version®), copyright © 2001 by Crossway, a publishing ministry of Good News Publishers. Used by permission. All rights reserved.

Manufactured in Dongguan, China/055760/416282

5 6 7 8 9 10 11 12 13 14   31 30 29 28 27 26 25 24 23 22

Foreword

This book is one of a series of six designed to help parents communicate biblical values to their children in the area of sexuality. *Where Do Babies Come From?* is the second book in the series. It is written especially for children ages six to eight and, of course, for the parents, teachers, and other concerned grown-ups who will read the book to the child.

Like its predecessor, this updated Learning about Sex series provides information about the mental, emotional, physical, and spiritual aspects of human sexuality. Moreover, it does so from a distinctively Christian point of view, in the context of our relationship to the God who created us and redeemed us in Jesus Christ. The series presents sex as another good gift from God that is to be used responsibly. To counter cultural influences, be strong and consistent in communicating the miracle of God's design. The way God made us is just the way He knew it should be for our health and happiness.

Each book in the series is graded—in vocabulary and in the amount of information it provides. It answers the questions that persons at each age level typically ask. Because children vary widely in their growth rates and interest levels, parents and other concerned adults will want to preview each book in the series, directing the child to the next graded book when he is ready for it.

In addition to reading each book, you can use them as starting points for casual conversation and when answering other questions a child might have. We pray that this will be the beginning of ongoing open, honest, and intentional communication with your child regarding God's magnificent design.

This book can also be used as a mini-unit or as part of another course of study in a Christian school or church setting. Whenever the book is used in a classroom setting, it is important to let the parents know beforehand, since they have the primary responsibility for the sex education of their children. If used in a classroom setting, the books are designed for separate single-gender groups, the setting most conducive to open conversations about questions and concerns. As the Christian home and the Christian school and church work together, Christian values in sex education can be more effectively strengthened.

The Editors

A Note to Grown-ups
about Communicating Values at Home

In story form, this book answers questions about sexuality that six- to eight-year-olds typically ask—or wonder about. Many children this age will have difficulty reading the book on their own, so plan to enjoy reading it with your child. Depending on his interest, read all of it at one time, or read one chapter at a time.

Make it just another book that you enjoy reading to or with your child at the usual times when you read together. Once you've read it, of course, you may want to read it again—next month or even next year, when your child is at a different developmental level and able to absorb more of the content.

Take your time as you read, expanding on the text when your child asks for further information. Most of all, use the occasion to wonder at the beauty and design of God's good gift of sexuality. After all, what we're most interested in is helping your child develop a reverent, wholesome, responsible attitude about human conception and birth and the way God made us male or female. We want to communicate not only truthful and accurate information about sexuality, but especially a deep appreciation of God's marvelous design and purpose and a sense of respect and responsibility toward all God has given. "God made me a boy— and His creation is wonderful!"

Here are six easy-to-remember guidelines (each beginning with a C) to keep in mind as you answer questions:

1. Commend your child for coming to you and for asking, especially if the question makes you uneasy! You want to keep the channels of communication open.

2. Clarify the question: "When you ask, 'Where do babies come from?' do you mean, 'How do they grow?'"

3. Communicate with simple, direct answers.

4. Connect your answer to what your child already knows (or thinks he knows): "Remember what you learned about . . . ? That will help you understand that . . ." Also, you may want to connect your child's question to other aspects of growing up, thereby avoiding the danger of isolating sex from the wider background of life in general.

5. Care must be taken to warn your child about the possibilities of abuse. You might want to work this into a discussion of appropriate behavior. "Your body belongs to you—including those private parts that your swimming suit covers. You don't show those parts or touch them in public. And other people should not touch your private parts either. No one has a right to do that unless it's a nurse or a doctor helping you to be well or someone who cares for you helping you to be clean. If anyone does touch your private parts, be sure to tell me. I want to keep you safe."

6. Christ Himself is with us and is guiding us in what we say and what we model about relationships. Share with your child: "Isn't it wonderful that Jesus, God's own Son, was born as a baby? He grew up—just as we do. So He knows what it's like when we feel lonely or afraid. He always did what was right—and He died on a cross—to pay for our sins. Now we can be sure that God, our Father, forgives us. And we can be glad that Jesus is there to help us grow as God's loving children."

Simon Has a Birthday

Simon was seven years old today. He could hardly wait to get home from school.

His dad, his mom, and his grandpa were all waiting. Grandpa always came over when there was a birthday or something else special.

"You need me to help you celebrate, don't you?" he said with a wink. Simon agreed as he gave him a hug. Then Simon saw his birthday cake.

"O-o-oh, it's cool!" he said. And it was! It had seven blue candles and seemed like it could be seven layers high! With the family gathered around, he opened his presents. There was a set of action figures, a pair of rollerblades, the game he had wished for, and tickets to go to the amusement park today.

"How did everyone know just what I wanted?" Simon wondered. "They must know me pretty well."

After Simon blew out the candles, his dad picked him up and gave him a bear hug. Simon giggled when he got his breath.

"Look how big our boy is getting, Mother," Dad said. "Do you still remember how he looked seven years ago today?"

"Seven years ago, Simon, you had just been born," Mother said. "You looked beautiful to me! Maybe you were just another red and wrinkled baby to some people. But to me, you were perfect! I wondered how your fingers and toes could be so tiny. I saw that you had your dad's brown eyes. And I prayed, 'Thank You, God, for such a fine baby.'"

"Yep," said Dad. "We thought you were really something special. Crying loudly, but very special! We were so glad God gave you to us. And wow! Did you change our family!"

"I changed our family?" Simon was surprised. "How could I do that? I was just a baby."

"Just a baby?" Dad laughed. "Before you came, Simon, there was just Mother and I to love each other. But after you came, we had another person to love. Soon you learned to love and trust us too. So then there was a lot more love in our family than ever before."

"You mean each new baby brings more love to a family?" Simon asked. When Mother nodded, Simon said, "Then every baby does change a family."

"That's right," Mother said. "Families are always changing. They change in different ways. A family grows larger whenever a baby is born or a child is adopted. And people in the family are always growing older, and the babies are always growing bigger."

"I know a family where the children are teenagers," Dad said. "They've grown taller than their mother and father."

"They'll be grown up soon," Simon said. "When they move away, that will make their family smaller again."

"That's what happened to our family," Grandpa said. "Our children got married. Then Grandma and I were a small family again."

"Sometimes a family may have just a father or a mother. Or a family can grow larger when grandparents come to live with them," Mother said.

"Why don't you come and live here with us, Grandpa?" Simon asked. "Then our family would grow again."

"Someday," Grandpa said, "maybe I will make this family grow bigger. Just like you did, Simon, when you were born. When I first saw you, I knew for sure you belonged in this family. That straight, firm nose is your mother's, for sure."

"But how did I get her nose, Grandpa?"

"Well, babies born into a family often look like someone else in their family. Of course, God doesn't make exact copies when He makes a new person. He makes each of us special—like no one else in the world."

"But what about John, next door?" Simon said. "I wonder why he doesn't look like anyone in his family."

"That's because he was adopted into his family," Dad explained. "He was born to another mother. She loved him but could not take care of him. John's parents wanted someone just like him for their family, so they adopted him."

"What does that mean—*adopted* him?" Simon asked.

"Well, Simon, it means they decided to make him their own child. They love him as much as if he were born to them."

"That's another kind of family!" Simon said.

"Families are different in many ways," said Mother. "Some families have just a mother or a father. Some families have only one child. Some families have many children.

"But in some important ways we are all the same. We are all people

- loved by God all the time,

- loving one another all the time,

- living and working together,

- doing things for one another,

- celebrating good times together,

- helping one another through bad times, and

- caring about what happens to one another."

"It was God who thought of putting us into families," Dad said. "Wasn't it a good idea? God knew that our family should start off with your mother and me, promising to love each other our whole lives. It was God's perfect plan that our family would grow to include you. We promise we'll always love you too."

"I'm glad God put me into this family," Simon said. "It's just right for me. God knows what I want. He knows me so well!"

"O families of the peoples, ascribe to the Lord glory and strength!" (Psalm 96:7)

A Trip to the Museum

"Well, I think I'm ready," said Mother. "Shall we go now?"

Simon was so excited! He was going to the museum with Mother and Dad. It was a special treat. They had promised Simon that he could take his friend Brenna along too.

In the car, Dad asked, "Well, Simon, what are we going to see first?"

"Oh, the baby chicks are hatching!" Simon didn't have any trouble deciding that. "They are my favorite thing in the whole museum." And he told them all about the little, fuzzy, yellow chicks sitting under the light to keep warm.

At last they were going up the steps of the museum. "Look, Mom, a balloon man! May I have a blue one? Please?"

"Okay," said Mother as she paid for the balloon. "But when will I ever get to see those chicks?"

"Come on, they're right over here," said Brenna.

"Look at this," Simon whispered. One little chick was just pecking through its eggshell. Simon was so excited he almost stopped breathing. Peck! Peck! They could all hear the tiny sounds from inside the egg. They watched quietly until the eggshell fell apart.

"Ooh, look at how wet and tired he is!" Brenna said. "Now he'll have to sit and rest until his feathers start to dry and get fluffy."

"I know babies don't hatch like chicks do," Simon said softly. "But I wonder just how they do get born."

"H-m-m-m," Dad said. "That's a big question."

"If you are finished watching the chicks," Mother said, "we may be able to find out over there by that blue sign."

"Oh! Look how tiny that baby is!" said Brenna. "I've never seen a baby that little."

"Hardly anyone does! When a baby is that tiny," Mother explained, "it can't eat or even breathe for itself. It has to live inside its mother's body. God made a special place for a baby to grow. It's called a womb. It's a cozy, warm, comfortable place that protects and takes care of the baby while it's so small. It is also called a *uterus*. That's usually what doctors call it."

"A *you-ter-us*?" The word sounded strange, but it wasn't hard to say.

GROWTH STAGES IN THE UTERUS

2 months

3 months

4 months

6 months

8 months

Brenna asked, "What is the uterus like? Is it like a little box?"

"More like a little balloon," Mother said. "Look, I'll show you." She took Simon's balloon, let some air out until it was about the size of a pear, and said, "It's just about this size. And it's hollow inside too."

"The tiny baby settles down near the side. The side of the uterus is much thicker than this balloon. That is where the baby grows."

"Here's a baby when it is bigger. Look!" Brenna said. "See those little fingers and those tiny little toes! And look at that little mouth."

Simon wondered aloud, "Can a baby eat with such a little mouth?"

"No, it can't eat when it is so tiny," Mother explained. "It doesn't need to eat while it's in the mother's uterus."

"The baby gets its food from the mother's body. See that cord going from the baby's tummy to the side of the uterus? Food from the mother's body comes to the baby's body through that cord so the baby can keep growing. The baby can't breathe yet either, so oxygen comes through that tube too."

"Was I ever so little that I couldn't breathe?" Simon wondered.

"You sure were!" Dad said. "Even somebody as big as me was that small once."

"It was a good thing you both had a mother to be connected to," said Mother. "Do you know where your cord joined your body, Simon?"

"Right in the middle somewhere, I guess," Simon answered with a little giggle. "At my belly button?"

"That's right!" Dad chuckled. "Sounds like you were buttoned onto your mother. The real name for that place is *navel*."

9 months

Another thing seemed strange to Simon. "I wonder why these babies don't have any clothes on," he said.

"They don't need clothes," Mother said. "It's so warm and comfortable in the uterus."

"And how can they ever go to the bathroom?" Brenna asked.

"Well, God had that all figured out too. You see the area around the baby, inside the uterus? The baby is actually floating in liquid that is mostly water. Not only does the water feel like a squishy cushion, but the baby can even urinate right into that water," Mother pointed to the *amniotic fluid*. "That water takes care of a lot of things. It keeps the baby warm, it protects the baby, and it even handles the baby's waste."

"Oh, wow!" Simon said. "But it must get pretty crowded in there when the baby gets bigger."

Dad laughed. "It is cozy, all right. The baby has to lie all curled up, with its legs bent and tucked under its chin."

"Look how big this next baby is!" Simon said. "Is there still enough room for such a big baby?"

"Bring me your balloon a minute," Dad said. "What would happen to this balloon if you blew more air into it?"

"I guess it would get bigger," Simon said.

"That's the answer," said Dad.

"You mean the uterus gets bigger like a balloon?"

"That's right," Mother said. "God designed a woman's body in an amazing way.

"As the baby grows, there's always room for it. When the baby grows this big, the mother's body becomes big and round. Then everyone can see that the mother has a baby growing in her."

"You mean she gets bigger, like Grandpa?"

"No, no," Mother said. "It's not the same as being overweight. We say she is *pregnant*. After the baby is born, the uterus will slowly go back to its normal size again, just like when air goes out of a balloon!"

"How does the baby get born then? Does the uterus break open like when a balloon gets popped?"

"Oh, no, Simon," Mother said. "The uterus has an opening something like a balloon has. That opening can stretch too. When it is time for the baby to be born, it comes out through the opening."

"Is that how I was born?" Simon asked.

"Yes, Simon," Mother said. "That's how you were born. That is God's special way of bringing new people into the world. Sometimes things happen that make it harder and less safe for a baby to come out through a mother's vagina, so doctors have to help the baby in a different way. But yes, that's God's wonderful design!"

"I don't understand it, but if it's God's plan, I think it must be the way it should be. Don't you think so, Dad?"

Dad agreed. "It is amazing. That's why they call it 'the miracle of birth.' And you thought learning about the way chicks are born was neat. God made you even more special than that!"

"I praise You, for I am fearfully and wonderfully made." (Psalm 139:14)

Boys and Girls—Fathers and Mothers

"Hey, Simon!" Someone was calling. Simon looked outside. Brenna and her little brother, Evan, were running through the rain to his porch.

"Can we play at your house?" they wanted to know.

"Sure," Simon said. "Come on in. What do you want to play?"

"Well, we can't play ball, because it's raining," Brenna said. "Besides, I have to take care of Evan. You know what four-year-old kids are like!"

"What can we play?" asked Simon.

"I want to play house," said Evan. "Can I be the mother? I want to cook." Evan picked up a bowl from the kitchen counter and he pretended to stir it with a big spoon.

Brenna and Simon laughed. "You can't be the mother, Evan," Simon said. "You're a boy! Boys and girls can be cooks. But only girls can be mothers."

Evan wasn't sure about this. "But I can be anything I want when I get big," he insisted. "Dad said I could!"

"Your dad meant that you could be an airplane pilot, or a firefighter, or even a cook," Simon explained. "He didn't mean you could be a mother. Only girls can be mothers."

"That's right," Brenna chimed in. "God made girls with a special place where a baby can grow inside them." Brenna patted her tummy.

"I wonder why it's in their stomach." Evan looked puzzled. "With all the hot dogs and pancakes and ice cream?"

"It's not in the woman's stomach. It's in a special place called the uterus," Brenna said. "It's inside the body, so you can't see it."

"If you can't see it," Evan said, "how do you know I don't have one too?"

"No way, Evan," said Simon. "I know for sure you don't, because you are a boy. Boys have their own special body. They grow up to be fathers."

"You mean boys have to be fathers?" Evan sounded confused. "Can't I be a cowboy when I am big?"

"Of course, Evan," Brenna laughed. "You can be a father as well as a cowboy or almost anything else you want to be."

"Oh, I'm so lucky," Evan sang. "Boys can be more things than girls."

"That's not what I said, Evan." Brenna was tired of explaining everything. "Girls can be many things too. I can be a mother and a lot of other things. I can be a teacher, a firefighter, or even a doctor. Boys and girls are different, but one is not better than the other."

"We can learn about this from God. He loves us all the same, boys and girls, men and women," said Simon. "From Jesus, we learn to treat all people with loving kindness and respect, whoever they are."

"Well, okay. Then I'll be the father," Evan decided. "But I still want to be the cook too. I'm going to make some hamburgers," he said, pretending to flip burgers on the grill.

"Male and female [God] created them, and He blessed them." (Genesis 5:2)

In Mother's Workroom

"Mother, where are you?" Simon called when he got in the house. He was hungry.

"I'm here in the workroom," Mother answered. "Why don't you get a cookie and come and talk with me a while?"

I wonder how she knew I wanted a cookie? Simon thought. Then he called, "May I have two, please?"

"Okay, Simon," Mother answered. "But put the lid back on the cookie jar."

"M-m-m! These are good," Simon said when he got to the workroom. "Thanks a lot."

"You sure had fun with Evan and Brenna yesterday," Mother said as she arranged some silk flowers.

"Uh-huh," Simon said. "I like playing with Brenna and Evan. But Evan sure says some funny things."

"Like what?" Mother asked as she attached the flowers to a wreath.

"Well," Simon said with his mouth full of cookie, "Evan wondered why he couldn't be a mother. And he complained that babies are always messy and crying."

"Well, they do cry a lot. But that is the only way they can tell someone they're hungry or hurt or cold," Mother said gently, as she added some berries to the wreath.

"You mean crying is like their way of talking?" Simon was surprised at that.

Mother nodded. "If they could say, 'Mommy, I want my diaper changed,' they wouldn't have to cry, would they?"

"I guess not," Simon said. "Are babies a lot of trouble?" he wondered out loud.

Mother laughed as she put her wreath down. "Babies do need care. But lots of people still want babies because they add so much joy to families. Why do you think people like babies?" She snipped off a piece of ribbon and began to make a fancy bow.

"Because babies are cute. And it's fun to take them on walks in their stroller," Simon said. "I see Anne doing that with her baby sister. And her baby sister laughs so hard when Anne plays peekaboo with her." Simon imagined what it would be like to do that with his new baby sister or brother.

Mother said, "I'm glad I wanted a baby a long time ago. Now I have my seven-year-old Simon to keep me company. What about you, Simon? Will you be happy when we have a new baby in our family?"

"Yeah . . . but I kind of like being the only kid in this family." Simon wasn't sure they needed any more kids. "I hope you'll still have time to play with me after we get a new baby," he said.

Mother pushed away the wreath she was working on and gave Simon a big hug.

"I've told you many times how much I love you. You will always be my boy, Simon. You don't ever have to be afraid that I won't have time for you. I like to do things with you. And you are getting so big now. You do so many things for yourself—like taking a bath and hanging up your clothes. Why, you're big enough to help Dad and me take care of our new baby."

Simon still wasn't sure. He looked at his mother. "It's hard to believe a baby is growing in you right now. What do you think? Will the baby be a boy or a girl?"

"We don't know yet. But soon the doctor will do a test that will be able to tell us," Mother said. "But one thing we know now is he or she can kick!"

"Is the baby kicking now?" Simon asked.

"Yes, Simon," Mother said. "Put your hand right here and you can feel the baby moving."

"Ooh, I can," Simon said. "The baby is really moving."

"Isn't that exciting?" Mother said as she gave Simon a little squeeze.

Simon had lots to think about as Mother flipped the wreath over to fasten a hook on the back. "Will the baby have to sleep in my room? I don't think there would be room for another bed. I know how much baby stuff Anne's little sister has. My room could get crowded."

"Oh, no." Mother held up the finished wreath to admire. "The baby will have this room! All my crafts will be moved to the basement. Would you like to see the new curtains I bought for the baby's room?"

Mother held up the curtains for Simon to see. "These curtains will be just right for a baby's room, don't you think? We'll put them up when Dad finishes painting the walls. He said you could pick out the color. What color do you think would look nice with these curtains?"

Simon thought yellow would, because there were little yellow ducks all over the curtains. Mother thought that was a good choice too.

"I bet I know what the baby will sleep in—my baby crib!" Simon was starting to get a little excited about getting ready for a new baby. "Can we get my crib down from the attic?"

"Not so fast!" Mother slowed him down. "It will be quite a while before the baby gets here. It will be about four months yet. Time enough to finish this room. We'll have to buy some new baby clothes too."

"Can I make something for the baby?" asked Simon, "Maybe a picture or a toy?" While he was thinking about what he would make, Mother got out the vacuum to clean up the rug. When the vacuum finally stopped, Simon asked another question. "Did the baby start growing a long time ago?"

sperm and egg

"Quite a while ago. It takes a baby nine months of growing before it is ready to be born. That's just as long as it took you to go through first grade."

"But what started the baby?" Simon wanted to know.

"That's another miracle. God planned it so that it takes both a mother and a father. You see, every baby begins when two very tiny parts join together and start to grow. You'd need a microscope to see them. One of these parts comes from the mother's body. It is called the *ovum* or the egg."

"An egg? Like a chicken egg?" Simon wondered, trying to make sense of it all.

"Well, yes, it is similar to mother hens laying eggs," Mom explained. "And the part that comes from the father's body is called the *sperm*. It's also called a seed."

"You mean daddies help babies start?" Simon was getting another surprise.

"Of course," Mother pinched his cheek. "You are Dad's boy too, aren't you?"

Simon laughed, "That's what he says every time he swings me around and around. But how do daddies help babies start? It's like planting a seed and growing something?"

"When a husband and wife love each other, they show it in many ways," Mother began.

"I know, they kiss each other and hug."

"That's right," said Mother. "They like to do things for each other, and they want to be together always and become a family."

"Is that why a bride and groom get married?"

"Yes, God is happy when two people decide to get married and start their life together with His blessing," Mother continued. "He made them for living together and showing their love to each other all their lives. During private times, they will kiss and hug, and they will also bring their bodies together very close and in a very special way. God made their bodies so they fit together. This is more than just a close hug.

"When a husband and wife join their bodies together, the sperm from the man's body can go into the woman's body. Sometimes a sperm and an egg join in the mother's body. That is when a new baby begins. A fertilized egg begins to grow a baby! Only together can they make a baby."

"And that's why a baby belongs to both its father and its mother!" Now Simon understood.

"Yes, that's the way God planned it! Both mother and father have a part in making the baby, but God has the biggest part. God blesses the mother and father and this new life as it grows and grows.

"It's sad that sin has ruined God's perfect plan, so that sometimes the mom and dad don't live together anymore, but God loves and blesses each family. He always knows just what's best for us, and He blesses us with everything we need, including forgiveness of our sins. And I'm so glad He's blessed our family with you and your new little brother or sister!"

"Praise the LORD . . . He blesses your children within you." (Psalm 147:12–13)

Dad Is Home

"So this is where my family is!" Dad was home. "Have you two been hiding on me—or should I say three?" he asked.

"Three?" Simon wondered why Dad said that. Then he said, "Oh, I know what you mean. We've just been talking about the baby."

"Good! And what have you ordered? A boy or a girl?"

Simon had to think about that. "We don't know that yet. But we will know for sure when we see it."

"Oh, really?" Dad laughed. "And how will you know then?"

"Because a baby boy's body is like his daddy's. And baby girl's body is like her mommy's. Right?"

"That's right!" said Dad. "Both boys and girls have the body parts they need to become fathers or mothers when they grow up."

"But what are those parts?" Simon wanted to know.

Mother answered, "When a baby girl is born, she already has the female parts she needs. A girl's uterus, you know, is inside her body. And she has a *vagina* that connects the uterus with the outside at an opening between the one for urine and the place for bowel movements."

"If girls have the female parts they need to become a mother someday, what parts do boys have so they can become fathers when they grow up?" asked Simon.

"Well, on the boy's body," Dad said, "the male parts you can see are the penis and the scrotum. The part that looks a little like a finger is called the *penis*."

"That is where the urine comes out," Mother explained. "Also, when a boy becomes a man, at certain times sperm will pass out through the penis."

"The *scrotum* is the sac behind the penis," Dad continued. "The scrotum holds the *testicles*. After a boy grows up, the testicles start making the sperm I told you about."

"Boys and girls are really different," Simon said. "I wonder which is the most important."

"There are many ways in which boys and girls are the same," Mother reminded him. "They both can grow, think, feel, and love. It is interesting that God planned for just about the same number of boys and girls to be born. So both of them must be important to Him."

"It's not a matter of being more or less important. Boys and girls, men and women, are different. And we need one another. At creation, God made Eve for Adam. Families help one another and share and care for one another. They love one another no matter what," said Dad. "This is God's plan for our lives. I can't imagine my life without your mother!"

"Thanks, " Mother smiled and hugged Dad. "Yes, God's plans are always good, especially His plan to care for us through Jesus, who forgives us and saves us. God's plans are more than good; they are perfect!"

"See what kind of love the Father has given to us, that we should be called children of God." (1 John 3:1)

Loving and Caring for One Another

"Simon," Mother called, "will you please come and set the table for supper? It's almost time to eat."

"Coming!" Simon followed the good smells into the kitchen. As he put the knives and forks beside the plates on the table, a big, round pizza came steaming out of the oven. It smelled delicious! Mother poured the milk and told Simon to call Dad to supper.

"I'm as hungry as a bear," Dad said as he sat down and put his napkin on his lap.

"Me too," Simon echoed. "Well, maybe as hungry as a bear cub," he smiled.

When everyone was sitting down, they folded their hands to pray: "Thank You for this food, Lord. You are good and Your love lasts forever. Bless these gifts You give us from Your mercy through Jesus. Amen."

"Is the new baby one of God's gifts to us?" Simon asked as soon as he had helped himself to a piece of pizza.

"The baby will be God's gift to all of us in this family and to so many others," Dad agreed. "We will all enjoy the baby. Everyone in the family can help take care of it too."

"Isn't it the mothers who take care of the babies?" Simon asked.

As Dad cut another piece of pizza for him, he said, "Fathers and brothers and sisters can all help keep babies clean and comfortable and make them feel happy and loved."

"Did you help take care of me when I was a baby?" Simon asked his dad as he took a big drink of milk.

"Did I ever!" Dad remembered. "When you were little, you had tummy aches almost every night after supper. I used to put you on your tummy and lay you on my lap. I'd bounce you a little, then pat you a lot. That seemed to be the only thing that would make you stop crying."

Simon wanted to help take care of the baby too. "Will I be able to hold the baby on my lap?"

"Sure, you'll be able to hold the baby," Dad promised, "as long as it doesn't wiggle too much."

"Will I be able to feed it too?" Simon wondered.

"No, not at first," replied Mother. "Newborn babies need only milk, and I plan to nurse the new baby just as I did you."

"You mean you're going to be the nurse if the baby gets sick?"

"No, no!" laughed Mother. "I should have explained that word *nurse*. When babies are born, their mothers have milk in their breasts to feed them. This is how God provides just the kind of food the baby needs. The baby snuggles close to the mother's breast and drinks the milk and feels very much loved."

"Babies don't know very many things when they are born," said Dad, "but no one has to teach them how to suck. They know that! They suck on fingers and pacifiers. They suck almost anything they can get into their mouths."

Simon laughed at that; then he remembered, "Anne's little sister drinks from a bottle with a nipple on it. I wonder why she gets her milk that way."

Mother knew about that too. "Some mothers feed their babies milk from bottles. That milk helps them grow strong and healthy too. Those mothers also love their babies very much. They hold them close, cuddle them, talk to them, and smile at them."

"You and I will be able to help feed the baby later, Simon," Dad said, "when it is ready for cereal and fruit juice and baby food."

"And we can talk to it and play with it and love it!" said Simon.

"We sure can," Dad said as he playfully tickled Simon. "And that's a very important part. That's what families are for—working together and loving one another, each in our own special way. It's all part of God's plan. Moms and dads and children all share their lives together. We love one another no matter what!"

Simon smiled and said, "What a special blessing it will be when this baby is born into our family and is born into God's family too!"

"Jesus said, 'Let the little children come to Me . . .
for to such belongs the kingdom of heaven.'" (Matthew 19:14)